MW01046980

The
COUNTRY POTTERY
Companion

The
COUNTRY POTTERY
Companion

Jocasta Innes
Photography by James Merrell

CollinsPublishersSanFrancisco
A Division of HarperCollinsPublishers

The Country Pottery Companion
Jocasta Innes

First published in USA in 1995
by Collins Publishers San Francisco
1160 Battery Street, San Francisco CA 94111

First published in Great Britain in 1995 by Mitchell Beazley
an imprint of Reed Consumer Books Limited

Photography by *James Merrell*
Illustrations by *Michael Hill*

Art Editor *Peta Waddington*
Editors *Sophie Pearse and Jonathan Hilton*
Art Director *Jacqui Small*
Executive Editor *Judith More*
Production *Heather O'Connell*

Library of Congress Cataloging-in-Publication Data
Innes, Jocasta
The country pottery companion/Jocasta Innes: photography by James Merrell.
   p. cm.
"First published in Great Britain by Mitchell Beazley"--T.p. verso.
Includes index.
ISBN 0-00-255491-7
1. Pottery--Collectors and collecting.   2. Ceramics in interior
decoration. 3. Decoration and ornament, Rustic.   I Title
NK4230,156   1995
738.3'075--dc20   94-38088
                                   CIP

The publishers have made every effort to ensure that all instructions given in this book are accurate and safe, but
they cannot accept liability for any resulting injury, damage or loss to either person or property, whether direct or
consequential and howsoever arising. The authors and publishers will be grateful for any information which will assist
them in keeping future editions up to date.

Colour reproduction by Rival Colour, UK
Produced by Mandarin Offset
Printed and bound in China

CONTENTS

INTRODUCTION

POTTERY MAKING IS THE OLDEST, CONTINUOUS HANDICRAFT OF WHICH WE HAVE EVIDENCE. THERE IS AN UNBROKEN STRAND THAT LINKS THE EARLIEST AND THE MOST RECENTLY MADE POTS, SINCE MANY OF THE TECHNIQUES EMPLOYED TODAY ARE IN FACT THOUSANDS OF YEARS OLD.

The overwhelming majority of pottery has always been made to fulfil honest, domestic functions – as containers, for storage, or simply plates to eat off. However, the craftsman's desire to stamp his work with something of himself, the innate urge to create beauty through texture, form, and surface decoration, to extend the medium beyond the known boundaries at any particular point, have created not only a desirable artform of immense charm, but also a unique historic record of the aesthetic aspirations and spiritual beliefs of humanity down through the millennia.

As the popularity of collecting pottery grows, antique or merely old pieces become increasingly hard to find. Attractive examples tend to migrate, perhaps as souvenirs or presents brought home by travellers and tourists. If the price is not scandalous, seize the chance to buy in foreign ware because opportunities are becoming fewer and further between.

EARTHENWARE

POTTERY

Traditional Earthenware

*E*ARTHENWARE IS A GENERALIZED TERM DESCRIBING ANY TYPE OF VESSEL, POT OR ORNAMENTAL OBJECT MADE OF BAKED CLAY. Perhaps the best-known form of earthenware is terra cotta, the traditional country-style red earthenware people most readily associate with plant pots, roofing tiles, a variety of architectural details, and some types of country kitchenware such as bread crocks and cooking vessels. The term "terra cotta" comes from the Italian, meaning "baked earth", and the clay itself contains up to about 10 percent of iron oxide, which gives this material its distinctive color.

Above: *Large terra cotta containers with lids provide cool storage space.* **Opposite:** *Glazed earthenware pieces have a natural dignity which makes them ideal for country cooks.*

The majority of other types of earthenware have a more neutral white-, gray-, or buff-colored base after firing, and it is these types of earthenware that are most suitable for decorative opaque glazes and slip decoration. Increasingly popular today is black earthenware, created by adding a special stain or manganese oxide to red clay.

Stoneware

THE TECHNIQUE OF MAKING STONEWARE, USING A BLEND OF CERAMIC MINERALS AND VERY PLASTIC CLAY, HAS BEEN KNOWN BY COUNTRY CRAFTS-MEN FOR HUNDREDS OF YEARS THROUGHOUT EUROPE, SCANDINAVIA, ASIA AND

Above: Sturdy stoneware bowls and pots fulfil a dual purpose; they can be used to store and to serve an ever-changing selection of foods.

THE NEW WORLD. Its origins, however are much older and are thought to be Chinese, where high-fired pottery dating back more than two thousand years has been found.

As its name implies, stoneware shares some characteristics with naturally occurring stone. These include a similar mineral composition and color (at least to some stones), a heaviness, denseness, and, most importantly, a non-porous nature.

When flicked, stoneware makes a characteristic ringing sound. The fineness or coarseness of the stoneware body is largely dependent on the temperature at which it is fired, which is normally around an extremely hot 2,400°F (1,300°C), as well as on the precise blend of clays and minerals employed.

And although the natural color range in stoneware pottery is not vast, it does have a fascinating textural range and a seemingly endless capacity for subtle variation within the natural, earthy hues that predominate.

Stoneware pottery can take on the heavily granulated texture of a lump of granite or the glassy smoothness of a slab of flawless slate, and just about anything in between. A common feature of this gutsy pottery, however, is the presence of specks and spots within the clay. These are caused when the extremely high firing temperatures required melt any impurities, such as iron or manganese, that may be present in the clay. Craftsmen have taken advantage of this characteristic by adding such "impurities" as rust filings, black sand, slag, copper and iron ores, iron pyrites, slate, chopped-up brick material, and small pieces of steel wool to the clay before it is fired to ensure a tough, gritty textured finish.

Below: A glazed stoneware pot makes a handy storage container for the country cook, while in front stands a Mexican tamale pot.

TRADITIONAL

POTTERY

Slipware

MOST PEOPLE'S NOTION OF POTTERY MAKING IS A COTTAGE SCENE WITH A LUMP OF AMORPHOUS CLAY RISING UPWARD THROUGH THE POTTER'S HANDS, TRANSFORMING AS THE WHEEL SPINS INTO A SATISFYINGLY USEFUL OBJECT. The potter's wheel is quite sufficient for the creation of one-off pieces, but it is not suitable for the production of more complicated and identical pieces of pottery; for this purpose a series of porous molds is used. Slip, which is a

mixture of clay and water, is poured into these molds and then a layer of clay is deposited on the inside surfaces. When firm, the components are removed and joined together.

Slip is also commonly used as a decorative medium. Mixed with coloring agents, it can then be applied to a piece of pottery in all kinds of different ways. In the hands of a skilled craftsman, slip decoration can be brushed on to a clay surface in order to give an effect similar to an oil painting. The slip may be piped on using a technique which is known as slip trailing, or alternatively it may be dabbed into place using a shaped piece of wood that has been dipped in slip. To produce even, overall color effects, pieces can be dipped directly into the mixture or, if preferred, the slip can be scratched away, before or after the firing stage, to form decorative patterns as the contrasting color of the clay base shows through. Slipware pots provide a useful adjunct in a kitchen, larder or pantry for storage space.

Right: The bold slipware patterns on bowls, pots and plates, and blocks of single-color slip decoration have become synonymous with country-style pottery. These slipware bowls have a buttery brown and cream glaze.

Opposite: Sitting comfortably on a wooden kitchen work surface, this lidded storage jar is decorated with slip-trailed yellow bands.

Saltglaze

THE TRADITIONAL PROCESS OF SALTGLAZING PRODUCES A FINISH THAT IS UNIQUE. It does, however, require a purpose-built kiln, one that cannot be used for making any other type of pottery. To produce the glaze, the clay body is heated at very high temperatures and, when it is red hot, wet salt is

Far left: *A trio of modern saltglazed jugs suspended from a ceiling; in this way they are stored out of the way and lend a decorative touch.* **Left:** *The high-gloss finish on this jug gives a unique translucency to the glaze.* **Opposite:** *A saltglaze pot provides an ideal container for the display and storage of bathroom accessories.*

added to the kiln. The sodium in the salt fuses with the clay – in the process, giving off highly dangerous hydrochloric acid fumes – to produce a translucent, shiny glaze that greatly enhances the form and surface texture of the clay object itself. If the clay body contains iron, then the glaze takes on an attractive irregular appearance, that resembles orange peel.

Spongeware

UNTIL THE AGE OF MASS PRODUCTION THAT WAS A MAJOR PART OF THE INDUSTRIAL REVOLUTION, AND THE ERA OF LOW-COST AND EFFICIENT COMMUNICATIONS AND TRANSPORTATION THAT ACCOMPANIED IT, POTTERY MAKING TENDED TO BE A LOCALIZED CRAFT SKILL. Commonly, pots would be traded, sold, or bartered to neighboring areas and some-

times far beyond, and techniques and design concepts did, therefore, spread out widely and cross-fertilize, but essentially each locality would have its own pottery tradition, produc-ing highly individualized pieces. So individual is a particular locality's pottery that archeolo-gists can date ancient sites, perhaps thousands of years old, on the evidence of pottery remains alone – the presence of a particular color, the shape of a handle or pouring lip, or the use of a certain design.

Although not all country potteries would necessarily have the skill, expertise or materials to produce classic pieces of earthenware or finer

Opposite: The country feel of this Victorian room is reinforced by the 19th-century spongeware plates and bowls displayed on a dresser. Above: An individual blue spongeware vase.

21

Above and opposite: A quirky rustic charm is the hallmark of traditional blue-and-white country spongeware, whether the pieces are grouped together or used as individual items.
Below: A brown-hued spongeware bowl and dried corn on the cob in dappled sunlight.

examples of porcelain, the desire to introduce ornamentation is a universal one. Where the artistic skill was lacking, decoration could be introduced by the application of spongeware patterns. These random splotches of color could be the principal decorative theme or they could be used as a broken ground for more figurative, life-like motifs.

Bright blues, mossy greens and pastels are common colors for spongeware decoration, which is applied by dabbing a sponge into colored slip – a creamy mixture of clay and water colored with minerals or pigments – and pressing it onto the clay body.

Spatterware

RELATED IN STYLE AND SPIRIT TO SPONGEWARE, SPATTERWARE IS ESSEN-
TIALLY AN AMERICAN POTTERY TRADITION. Much country-style pottery
tends to be rather crudely decorated, being produced for a
market that was essentially concerned with good value and practical

down-to-earth matters, and often
with little inclination to throw
money away on the passing fads,
fashions and changing tastes that
were more readily indulged in by
their urban counterparts.

To create this decorative
effect, the clay body of the bowl,
pot or mug would first of all be
dipped in a colored slip – most
likely a neutral white, cream, or
pastel – and then allowed to dry

Above and opposite: *The cheerful, rustic
charm of spatterware pottery is evident in these
attractive country-made pieces.*

and harden. Next, a contrasting color would be simply spattered over the
surface to create a random and eye-catching effect. The color would first
be loaded onto, say, a stiff-bristled brush and then just flicked.

Delftware

THE GREAT FLOWERING OF DELFTWARE TOOK PLACE BETWEEN THE MID 17TH AND MID 18TH CENTURIES. It is difficult to say why Delft itself – a small town just north of Rotterdam in Holland – became the center of this great pottery tradition. Its location near the extensive Dutch canal system would certainly have had a part to play, however, providing an easy export route for the finished ware as well as an import route for the fine-quality clay required. Another factor was a severe decline in the local brewing industry, which left many large buildings in Delft vacant.

These eminently suitable structures were eagerly taken over and converted by the potteries that soon began to flourish there, many of which adopted not only the premises but also the names of these former breweries.

The principal design influences on Delftware came from Italy and, of course, China. As more examples of the characteristically

Above: *A Chinese themed collection of blue-and-white Delftware pieces.* **Opposite:** *Manganese-purple Delftware. The purple was added to the unglazed, fired clay.*

blue-and-white Ming porcelain reached Europe, determination to match the quality and imitate the style of these oriental masterpieces grew. During this process Delftware developed its own unique identity, one based on the quality of its painting and a growing originality in the scenes and motifs depicted, which encompassed mythology, biblical scenes, portraits, and landscapes. Although blue and white is most often associated with Delftware, another style developed that used outlines rendered in manganese purple to give more definition to the drawing.

27

Blue & White

THE MING PERIOD WITNESSED A GREAT FLOWERING OF CHINESE NATIONAL PRIDE AND ARTISTIC ACHIEVEMENT. Returned at last to home rule after the demise of the Mongol Yuan dynasty, China under the Mings (1368-1644) has been compared with the Renaissance in Europe. One of the more significant introductions of the period occurred in the making of pottery and, especially, porcelain – that of blue underglaze painting on a white porcelain base. The ore used to produce this color – cobalt blue – may have been imported from Persia, although this is by no means certain. But as the period progressed, Chinese potters slowly learned how to extract a very pure form of the mineral, so removing the slightly degraded color evident in early Ming blue-and-white ware.

The striking contrast of the strong blue color against the thin, pure white base of the porcelain ensured this ware immense popularity, not only at the Chinese imperial court but also as an export product. Its influence can be seen most directly in much of the Dutch Delftware (see pp. 26-7) and in the English Willow pattern. Blue-and-white patterned pottery and porcelain became the mainstay of many English potteries

Opposite: This display in a sunshine yellow Hollywood kitchen demonstrates that blue-and-white china of different styles and periods has a natural affinity that makes it very collectible.

during the 18th century, using initially Chinese-inspired designs and motifs, but later branching out into design areas featuring more European themes – birds, flowers, figures and landscapes. To satisfy demand for blue-and-white ware, an innovation from the enamel industry was adopted – that of transfer-printing onto the porcelain. Production increased massively but, as a result, quality suffered enormously.

Above: A diverse collection of French blue-and-white ware. You can freely mix patterned china and pottery as long as they share a common blue-and-white color scheme.

The influence of blue-and-white ware, and especially its translation by the Delft potteries to suit the European export market and tastes, spread throughout that continent during the 18th century. From Austria and Germany much fine-quality work was produced – strapwork coupled with coats of arms, for example, vases with Chinese-inspired decoration, and much "useful", or not solely decorative, porcelain from

the Fulda pottery. In Scandinavia, the Danish king set up a factory that produced Delft-style pottery and in Sweden much blue-painted faïence – tin-glazed earthenware – was made during this period.

Numerous examples of Chinese porcelain had been finding their way in to and around Europe for some years prior to the 15th century, but it was during the 16th century that this trade greatly expanded and Italy became the main market. The majority of this porcelain was of the popular blue-and-white variety and it had an immense impact on the Italian production of maiolica, or majolica as it is also known, which attempted to imitate not only its coloring but also its porcelain base.

Right: An attractive contemporary variation on the traditional blue-and-white color theme using clays of different colors to produce a distinctive marbelized effect.

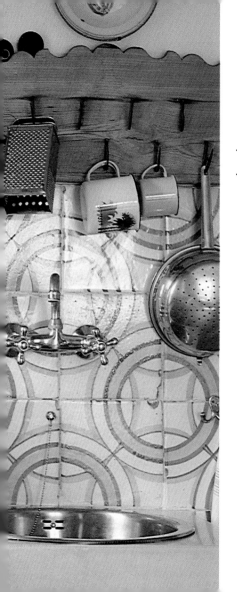

INTERNATIONAL

POTTERY

North American

THE NATIVE TRIBES OF NORTH AMERICA HAVE A LONG AND VARIED POTTERY TRADITION. Whereas the European philosophy sets humanity apart from the forces of nature, generally the native tribes of North America, and most other indigenous peoples of the world, tend to see themselves as an integral part of that process, and their art and culture, including their traditional pottery, as simply another manifestation of the natural world they perceive.

In very general terms, native North American pottery can be broken down into broad groups, including the Hohokam, Anasazi, and Mogollon, with most colorful and boldly patterned being the Anasazi. As well as making pots for ordinary domestic purposes, such as cooking and storage, pottery also formed an important part of the religious and spiritual life of many tribes. In this respect, there are innumerable examples of such ritual vessels as funereal pots, incense burners and braziers.

Opposite: The functional simplicity and clarity of design and color are what make these Navajo red and black luster pots such desirable and collectible objects today. *Above:* A rough-hewn wooden country-style dresser used to display a set of crockery made by the Wallace company, manufacturers of china for the hotel and restaurant trades, between 1938 and 1965.

Mexican

THE FOLK TRADITION OF POTTERY MAKING IN CENTRAL AMERICA IS KNOWN TO DATE BACK MORE THAN 5,000 YEARS. Although there is evidence that some Mexican pots were turned on a wheel, there were three traditional forms of pottery making: molding, coiling, and modeling. The standard of wares produced depended, as it does today, on the quality of the clay used, and in some locations this was very fine. Different methods of firing were employed to produce pottery ranging in color from red through gray, brown, and black and, at its best, the decoration – abstract or figurative – has been described as the most exquisite and sensitive found anywhere in the world.

Left: *Displayed on a tiled dining-room table inside a Spanish colonial house, these pieces of brightly colored, thick earthenware pottery are typical of everyday domestic wares. They are set against a backdrop of a scuffed painted cupboard and lend a modest, welcoming peasant style.* **Opposite:** *This selection of chunky, contemporary hand-painted crockery has a rough glaze in exuberant color.*

English

WITH ITS HISTORY AS ONE OF THE GREAT TRADING NATIONS, IT IS NOT SURPRISING THAT THERE IS SUCH A RANGE OF POTTERY STYLE AND TECHNIQUES TO BE FOUND IN ENGLAND. Earthenware products had been made since prehistoric times and Celtic pottery has a richness and variety of form with overtones of its Eastern and European origins. The names of English pottery styles bear witness to their places of origin, some producing domestic saltglazed stoneware while others fine-quality, ornamental porcelain. The engine that drove the English pottery industry was fuelled by two factors: the onset of the Industrial Revolution, which introduced new methods for mass-produced goods, and the expansion of its colonial empire, which ensured a ready market for the output of the famous Staffordshire pottery centers.

Right: *The names tell us all we need to know: striped Cornishware, a Staffordshire ware jug, and a spotted Dartmouth ware pot.*

Opposite: *A collection of quite disparate examples of English domestic ware, attractively displaying a diverse range of color, pattern, and style.*

French

Pottery from France has found its way into homes all over the world. Whatever your taste, some dish, bowl, pot, or platter is probably already installed in one room or another, whether it be the chunky Provençal ware decorated in buttery ocher or green glazes or the prettier, more delicate flower-strewn products from such French potteries as Quimper. The town of Quimper in Brittany had been an important regional center for hundreds of years, as its fine 15th-century cathedral testifies. The Quimper decorative pottery tradition was heavily influenced by the Rouen factory, which gained distinction from about the beginning of the 18th century through its characteristic use of "lambrequins" – a border pattern used on ceramics giving a draped effect – and radiating patterns of lacy designs, swags of flowers, and scrollwork based on motifs found on decorative ironwork of the period.

The Beauvais potteries are known to have produced the first non-porous stoneware products in France, from sometime toward the end of the Middle Ages. The quality of the Beauvais ware was so fine that it found ready export markets in the Low Countries as well as England. Moving through the 15th century, French techniques of making glazed pottery became increasingly refined, reaching their zenith in the 16th century. Such was the

Opposite: *The bright, strong colors and rich glazes of typical Provençal pottery.*

quality of the work from provinces like Normandy, Saintonge, and Beauvaisis that the popularity of this traditional French ware was not diminished even by a huge influx of Italian Renaissance pottery. During the 17th century, the amount of Chinese blue-and-white ware (see pp. 28-31) being imported prompted French potteries into action. With characteristic verve, French production – and quality – increased to the extent that its potteries dominated Europe for most of the 18th century.

Opposite: Examples of pottery from Provence in highly glazed colors of green, ocher and dark brown.
Below left and right: *Typical border patterns found on pottery from the Quimper pottery, Brittany, France, with the central motifs set against a pale-colored ground.*

![pottery icon]

Mediterranean

THE TYPE OF POTTERY MOST READILY ASSOCIATED WITH MEDITERRANEAN COUNTRY STYLE IS PROBABLY THAT FROM SPAIN AND ITALY. The colors of the landscape are bound to leave an indelible imprint on the work of craftsmen and artists of all types. In the Mediterranean region, the dominance of

Above left: *Mediterranean style found in the pottery of Provence.* **Above right:** *Plain and simple pottery.* **Opposite:** *Glazed Spanish tableware decorated in contrasting and strongly patterned slip.*

the robust, earthy reds and browns of the soil, the intense blue of the Mediterranean sea and cloudless skies, and the often startling green of the lush spring vegetation before the fierce sunshine of summer turns it more toward the burned russets of fall, can all be seen reflected in the pottery of

45

the countries making up this melting pot of East and West.

In Italy, the sunshine colors of the Mediterranean style of pottery can be seen in the decorative earthenware made from the 19th century onward. Its principal source of inspiration was the beautifully painted maiolica, or "majolica" as it is also spelled, of the Renaissance period. Notable examples originated from the Torquato Castellani pottery in Rome and the Torelli pottery

Above: *The colors of this simply glazed earthenware jug seem to mirror those of the landscape in which the potter lived and worked. Its origins are Italian and it is typical in shape and style of a rustic tradition.* **Opposite:** *The Mediterranean sun and sky has been transmuted into this maiolica-style pottery.*

in Florence. Also in Florence, toward the end of the 19th century, Ulysse Cantagalli was responsible for some of the best imitations of early maiolica.

Much of the 19th-century Spanish maiolica pottery – typified by potteries such as Escofet or Fortuny of Madrid – had its historical roots in the much earlier 15th- and 16th-century Hispano-Moresque ware. This ware consisted of luster decoration on a tin-enameled ground.

POTTERY

PATTERNS

Plain Glaze

THE CHARM OF THE CLAY IS OFTEN MORE PRONOUNCED WHEN IT IS LEFT FREE OF DECORATION, WITH JUST A SIMPLE GLAZE FOR DEFINITION AND PROTECTION. In fact, with few exceptions, such as pure terra cotta earthenware, even if completely unadorned the surface of the clay once fired is seldom absolutely "plain". Most clays contain a range of minerals, which, depending on the kiln temperature, melt and fuse in a random fashion to produce a variegated, often unpredictable surface finish. With non-porous stoneware, for example, potters take advantage of the high firing temperatures to add minerals and crushed ores to the clay knowing that they will melt and so enhance the textural qualities of the finished ware (see pp. 12-13).

Left: *Sturdy, plain and simple stoneware bowls and pots can be used as table accompaniments alongside many other styles of pottery. They are also endlessly useful for storing all kinds of kitchen cutlery and other implements, as shown here.* **Opposite:** *These plain-glazed cups and saucers have a timeless elegance that never dates or looks inappropriate. If you plan to use or collect sets of a particular design then you should always check how long they will remain in production in order to allow for replacement of any breakages.*

Floral

AN INCREASE OF INTEREST IN PLANT STUDIES AND PORTRAITS COINCIDED WITH A SIGNIFICANT "FLOWERING" OF PORCELAIN AND POTTERY PRODUCTION IN 18TH-CENTURY EUROPE. Some of the famous Chelsea studio's production in England was turned over to making crockery which was decorated with plant studies, while in other parts of Europe potteries were creating new and imaginative designs festooned with flowers and foliage in generous natural profusion. It was also during the 18th century that creamware with its characteristic border composed of vine leaves, roses, carnations, and other plant species made its first appearance.

During the 19th century, flower designs migrated from the borders to become instead overall patterns, a trend that continued into the 20th century with flower studies that were either realistic or else more stylized and abstract.

Right: This pine rack provides an ideal means of display for late 19th- and early 20th-century pieces. *Opposite:* Different styles of pottery blend well together within a decorative theme.

Animals

EVOCATIONS OF THE NATURAL WORLD ARE CONSTANT AND RECURRING THEMES IN COUNTRY-STYLE POTTERY. Archeological remains of pottery from mankind's earliest history provide a fascinating insight into the relationship between humanity and the animal world, wherein animals were variously regarded as representatives of the spirit world or afterlife, as deities in their own right, or as subjects to be revered and respected for their strength, courage, tenacity, or fleetness of foot. Examples abound from all of the great

civilizations of the past: Phrygian jugs from Anatolia painted in the 7th century BC with their typical animal representations; even earlier Egyptian pottery displaying portraits of their animal-inspired gods; Ancient Greek images of mythical

Left: Fish and crabs are the dominant theme of this friendly spongeware collection of plates and platters. Opposite: Country-inspired themes of animals including fish and roosters decorate this fresh-looking green and blue spongeware crockery, produced by the English potters Hinchcliffe and Barber.

animal creatures or highly realistic portraits of fish and octopuses on earthenware plates and storage vessels; Roman hunting scenes; Chinese images of birds, fish, and deer contrasted with other examples of impossible sea creatures and ferocious, coiling dragons. The symbolic and decorative potential of the animal world is endless.

In the more recent history of pottery, there are innumerable examples of tin- and lead-glazed pottery, salt-glazed stoneware, majolica and porcelain through the Middle Ages and into the Renaissance period featuring animal decoration and motifs. Moving on, rustic ware such as the Frenchman Bernard Palissy's dishes featuring three-dimensional snakes, lizards, and lobsters, 18th-century Chinese-inspired peacock designs from studios in Bristol and Lambeth in England, right through to both individual and mass-produced pottery today of domestic animals, which looks so apposite in a country-cottage setting.

Contemporary

MODERN, FUNCTIONAL, COUNTRY-STYLE POTTERY – RANGING FROM
UNGLAZED GRATIN DISHES TO BRIGHTLY PAINTED SERVING BOWLS – IS AVAIL-
ABLE FROM VIRTUALLY EVERY COUNTRY IN THE WORLD. Spongeware has a
popular appeal, whether in bright green and white from Italy or soft pastels
from England. As well as relatively mass-produced designs, there are hundreds of small potteries turning out one-offs or limited ranges of mugs and jugs, cups and saucers, plates and platters in a number of glazes and finishes. These are always worth taking an interest in, since any one of them could turn out to be tomorrow's Lucie Rie.

A recent trend is for bright, overall patterns, and many studios now commission work from modern designers for small runs of not-too-expensive pottery and ceramics.

Above: *The brightly painted background acts as the perfect complement for an explosion of color and pattern provided by a mantle shelf display of modern ceramics.* **Opposite:** *Boldly patterned crockery in strong colors is typical of contemporary design; these pieces are part of a hand-painted tartan service.*

DISPLAYING

POTTERY

Mix and Match

NO ROOM FOR THE PURIST WHEN IT COMES TO A COUNTRY COTTAGE DISPLAY OF DECORATIVE POTTERY. One of the most homey images we have of the "typical" country cottage is that of clutter, and at its heart is, of course, the kitchen – the natural place in which to put together a pottery collection. People have enjoyed collecting and displaying pottery for hundreds of years, and at every social level – from the goodwife trading eggs, cheese, and butter at market for sturdy slipware in brown and cream, to the 18th-century Swedish countess who fitted up her boudoir-cum-kitchen with a clutch of cherub brackets to display her blue-and-white Chinese export ware. Just how prized these pieces were can be gauged by the care with which broken treasures were rivetted so that the item could start a new life as a decorative item for the wall.

Opposite and right: Full to overflowing, these rooms, decorated in traditional Slavonic country style, radiate warmth and a welcoming friendship. Every shelf and free area of wall is covered with examples of decorative pottery.

Dresser Display

*C*OUNTRY-STYLE POTTERY NEEDS
TO BE SEEN, NOT LEFT TO LAN-
GUISH, GATHERING DUST IN THE
BACK OF A CUPBOARD. Generally
speaking, display dressers have
closed cupboards up to dado level,
for storing less presentable pieces of
china or pottery, and open shelving above reaching some way short of the
ceiling. This allows you to stand larger pieces on top. If open shelving is not
suitable, you can cage the shelving in with chicken wire or brass mesh, or use

glazed doors to front the display
shelves. Choose paint colors care-
fully to set off the decoration on the
pottery as attractively as possible.

*Above: This collection of novelty Portuguese
and Italian pottery is an eye-catching asset in
any kitchen. Left: A blue dresser beautifully
sets off an explosion of color and pattern.
Opposite: A warm ocher color has been chosen
for this dresser to act as a suitable backcloth to
a collection of modern pottery.*

Index